Name

नाम

Bulk copies of this book and permission to reproduce may be requested via email – contact@raisingworldchildren.com

Paperback ISBN   978-1-956870-15-2
ebook ISBN   978-1-956870-18-3

Learn more about Aditi Wardhan Singh and get the audio/video version of this book and other multicultural

READING GUIDE :

A book like this can be a wonderful resource for strengthening family bonds and improving language skills! Here are five ways to use it at home:

Daily Conversation Practice – Set aside time each day for kids to read and try out phrases with their grandparents, making conversations more natural.

Storytelling Sessions – Grandparents can use the book to spark discussions about their childhood, traditions, or life lessons, helping kids learn Hindi in a meaningful way.

Games & Role-Playing – Turn the book into a playful activity where kids act out dialogues, ask questions, or even teach grandparents new English words in return!

Bedtime Learning – Integrate language lessons into bedtime storytelling by reading phrases or short stories from the book together, making learning cozy and fun.

When would you say this? - Ask your child or think to yourself the context. Pay attention to the aa or ii in the end when referring to yourself, depending on gender. You can also address yourself as "hum" , which is much more formal.

A note :

In most Indian families, grandparents have special affectionate names. They differ slightly based on region, language, or family traditions or sub-cultures also.

Side / Language	Grandmother	Grandfather
Hindi – Maternal	Nani	Nana
Hindi – Paternal	Dadi	Dada
Tamil	Paati (maternal) / Ammamma (paternal)	Thatha (maternal) / Appa or Thatha (paternal)
Telugu / Kannada	Amma / Ammamma	Nanna / Thatha
Marathi	Aaji	Ajoba
Gujarati	Baa	Bapuji / Dada
Punjabi	Bibi / Dadi	Dada / Baba

Grow your Hindi language skills with Our Conversations Series

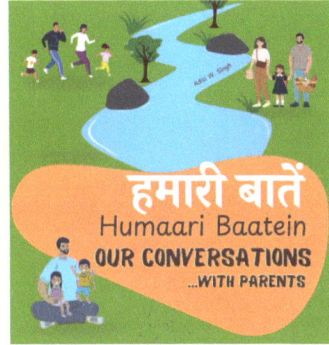

Menu

Greetings

नमस्ते दादा/दादी! आप कैसे हैं?

Namaste Dada/Dadi! Aap kaise hain?

Hello Paternal Grandpa/Grandma! How are you?

Nana/Nani

Maternal Grandfather/Grandmother

आपकी तबीयत कैसी है?

Aapki tabiyat kaisi hai?

How is your health?

आपने खाना खा लिया?

Aapne khaanaa khaa liya?

Have you eaten?

मैं आपकी मदद कैसे कर सकता/सकती हूँ?

Main aapki madad kaise kar saktaa/sakti hoon?

How can I help you?

2

हमें गोद में उठा लो।

Humein god mein uthaa lo.

Lift us in your arms.

आपको कुछ/पानी/दवाई चाहिए?

Aapko kuch/pani/dawaai chaahiye?

Do you want anything/water/
medicine?

Checking on Their Well-being

दादाजी, आपकी पीठ का दर्द अब कैसा है?

Dadadji, aapki peeth ka dard ab kaisa hai?

Grandpa, how is your back pain now?

दादीजी, क्या आपको दवा समय पर मिल रही है?

Dadiji, kya aapko dawaa samay par mil rahi hai?

Grandma, are you taking your medicine on time?

आज मौसम ठंडा है, आपको गरम कपड़े पहनने चाहिए।

Aaj mausam thandaa hai, aapko garam kapde pehnane chahiye.

It's cold today, you should wear warm clothes.

हम साथ में जूस पियें?

hum saath mein juice piyen?

Shall we drink juice together?

Expressing Care & Love

मुझे आपकी बहुत याद आती है।

Mujhe aapki bahut yaad aati hai.

I miss you a lot.

आपसे बातें करना मुझे बहुत अच्छा लगता है।

Aapse baatein karna mujhe bahut accha
lagta hai.

I love talking to you.

आप थक्क गये हो।
आप सो जाओ।

Aap thakk gaye ho.
Aap so jao.
You are tired. should
sleep.

आप जो भी बनाएंगी, मैं खुशी से
खाऊँगा/खाऊँगी।

Aap jo bhi banaayengi, main khushi
se khaunga/khaungi.
Whatever you cook, I'll happily eat
it.

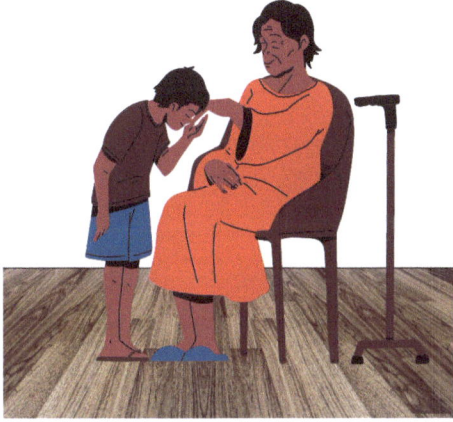

आपका आशीर्वाद हमारी सबसे बड़ी ताकत है।

Aapkaa aashirwad hamaari sabse badi taakat hai.

Your blessings are our greatest strength.

चलो कहीं साथ चलेगीं।

Chalo kahin saath chalein.

Let's go somewhere together.

Helping Them with Technology

दादा जी, मैं आपको वीडियो कॉल करना सिखा सकता/सकती हूँ।

Dadaji, main aapko video call karnaa sikhaa saktaa/sakti hoon.

Grandpa, I can teach you how to make a video call.

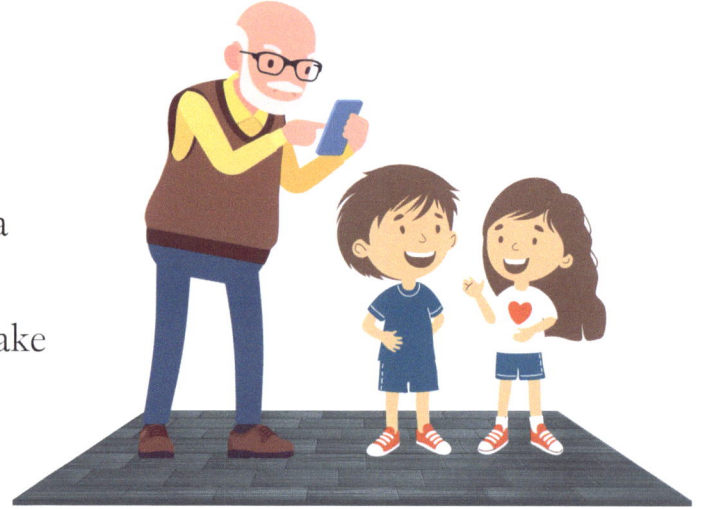

मैं आपके फोन में बड़ा फॉन्ट सेट कर दूँ?

Main aapke phone mein bada font set kar doon?

Should I set a bigger font on your phone?

अगर आपको कोई मैसेज भेजना हो, तो मुझे बताइए।

Agar aapko koi message bhejnaa ho, to mujhe bataaiye.

If you want to send a message, just let me know.

आपके फोन में कोई दिक्कत आ रही है?

Aapke phone mein koi dikkat aa rahi hai?

Is there any issue with your phone?

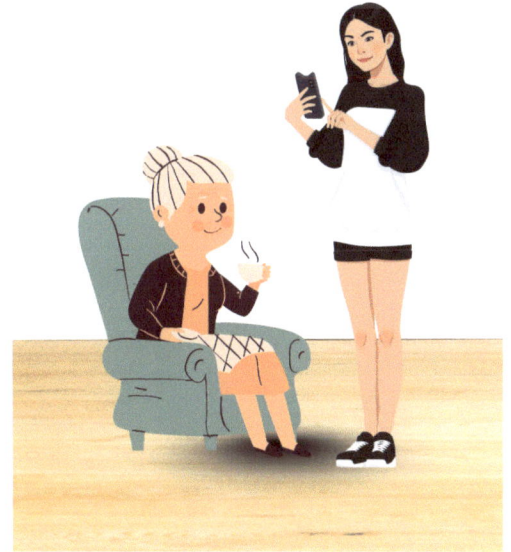

Spending Quality Time with Them

दादाजी, चलिए साथ में कुछ पुरानी तस्वीरें देखते हैं।

Dadaji, chaliye saath mein kuch puraani tasveerein dekhte hain.

Grandpa, let's look at some old photos together.

दादी,मुझे कोई कहानी सुनाओ ना।

Dadi, mujhe koi kahaani sunao na.

Grandma, tell me a story please.

आप हमें अपनी शादी/बचपन के बारे में बताइए।

Aap humein apni shaadi/bachpan ke baare mein bataiye.

Tell us about your wedding/childhood.

क्या आप मुझे कोई नया खेल सिखा सकते हैं जो आपने बचपन में खेला था?

Kya aap mujhe koi nayaa khel sikha sakte hain jo aapne bachpan mein khela tha?

Can you teach me a game you played in your childhood?

आपके समय में यह कैसा था?

Aapke samay mein yeh kaisa tha?

How was this in your time?

आपके अनुभव से मुझे बहुत कुछ सीखने को मिलता है। आपकी क्या राय है?

Aapke anubhav se mujhe bahut kuch seekhne ko miltaa hai. Aapki kyaa raay hai?

I learn a lot from your experiences. What is your opinion?

आज हम कुछ नया करते हैं.

Aaj hum kuchch nayaa karte hain.

Let's do something new today.

क्या आप हमारे साथ स्कूल चलेंगे?

Kyaa aap humaare saath school chalenge?

Will you come with us to school?

Festivals and Family

मिठाई खाई आपने?

Mithaai khaai aapne?

Did you eat the sweets?

मुझे पटाखे जलाने दो ना!

Mujhe pataakhe jalaane do na!

Please let me light the firecrackers!

नानाजी, पिचकारी भर दी? चलो रंग खेलते हैं!

Naanaaji, pichkaari bhar di? Chalo rang khelte hain!

Grandpa, did you fill the water gun? Let's play with colors!

दादी, आज आपको सबसे पहले रंग लगाऊँगा!

Daadi, aaj aapko sabse pehle rang lagaunga!

Grandma, I will put color on you first today!

तिलगुल खाओ, मीठा-मीठा बोलो!

Tilgul khao, meetha-meetha bolo!

 Eat sesame sweets and say sweet things!

(Common Makar Sankranti greeting)

मुझे भांगड़ा सिखाइए!

 Mujhe bhangra sikhaaiye!

 Teach me the Bhangra dance!

(Baisakhi/Lohri)

दादी, आज कितने पकवान बनाए आपने?

Daadi, aaj kitne pakwaan banaaye aapne?

Grandma, how many yummy dishes did you make today?

चलो पतंग उड़ाएँ!

Chalo patang udaayein!

Let's fly kites!

(Makar Sankranti special)

18

आशीर्वाद दो कि मैं अच्छे नंबर लाऊँ!

Aashirvaad do ki main acche number laaun!

Bless me so I get good marks!

दादा-दादी, ये त्यौहार आपके साथ ही मज़ेदार लगता है!

Daada-Daadi, ye tyohaar aapke saath hi mazedaar lagta hai!

Grandma-Grandpa, the festival is only fun with you!

अगले साल पक्का इंडिया में साथ सेलिब्रेट करेंगे!

Agle saal pakkaa India mein saath celebrate karenge!

Next year we will definitely celebrate in India together!

मिठाई पार्सल करके भेज दो!

Mithai parcel karke bhej do!

Send me some sweets in parcel!

Answering Common Questions

तुमने खाना खा लिया?

Tumne khana kha liya?

Have you eaten food?

✅ हाँ दादी/दादा, मैंने खा लिया।

Haan Dadi/Dada, maine kha liya.

Yes Grandma/Grandpa, I've eaten.

✅ अभी नहीं, लेकिन मैं जल्दी ही खा लूँगा/लूँगी।

Abhi nahi, lekin main jaldi hi kha loonga/loongi.

Not yet, but I'll eat soon.

तुम क्या खाना चाहोगे/चाहोगी?

Tum kya khaanaa chahoge/chahogi?

What would you like to eat?

✅ जो भी आप बनाएंगी, मुझे अच्छा लगेगा।

Jo bhi aap banayengi, mujhe acchaa lagegaa.

Whatever you make, I'll love it.

✅ आज कुछ हल्का और सादा खाना अच्छा लगेगा।

Aaj kuch halkaa aur saada khaanaa acchaa lagegaa.)

Something light and simple would be nice today.

✅ अगर आज पराँठे बनाएँ तो मज़ा आ जाएगा!

Agar aaj paraanthe banayein to mazaa aa jaayegaa!

 If you make parathas today, that would be amazing!

तुम हमारे साथ आ रहे/रही हो?

Tum hamaare saath aa rahe/rahi ho?)

Are you coming with us?

✅ हाँ, मैं तैयार होकर आता/आती हूँ।

Haan, main taiyyaar hokar aata/aati hoon.

Yes, I'll get ready and come.

✅ अभी नहीं, लेकिन आप जाइए, मैं बाद में आ जाऊँगा/जाऊँगी।

Abhi nahi, lekin aap jaayie, main baad mein aa jaaunga/jaungi.

Not right now, but you go ahead, I'll come later.

तुम कब वापस आओगे/आओगी?

Tum kab wapas aaoge/aaogi?

When will you be back?

✅ बस थोड़ी देर में लौट आऊँगा/आऊँगी।

Bas thodi der mein laut aaunga/aaungi.

 I'll be back in a little while.

✅ शाम तक वापस आ जाऊँगा/जाऊँगी।

Shaam tak wapas aa jaunga/jaungi.

I'll be back by evening.

तुम हमसे मिलने कब आ रहे हो?

Tum humse milne kab aa rahe ho?

When are you coming to meet us?

✅ बस दादी/दादा, आपकी याद बहुत आ रही है! जल्दी आने की पूरी कोशिश करूँगा/करूँगी।

Bas Dadi/Dada, aapki yaad bahut aa rahi hai! Jaldi aane ki poori koshish karunga/karungi.

Grandma/Grandpa, I miss you so much! I'll try my best to come soon.

✅ अगर आप कहें तो मैं अभी पैकिंग शुरू कर दूँ!

Agar aap kahein to main abhi packing shuru kar doon!

If you say so, I'll start packing right now!

✅ जल्दी ही आऊँगा/आऊँगी, लेकिन आप तब तक अपना ख्याल रखना!

Jaldi hi aaunga/aaungi, lekin aap tab tak apnaa khayaal rakhnaa!

I'll come soon, but until then, take care of yourself!

आप कहाँ जा रहे/रही हो?

Aap kahan jaa rahe/rahi ho?

Where are you going?

✅ मैं स्कूल जा रहा/रही हूँ, आपको कुछ लाना है?

Main school ja rahaa/rahi hoon, aapko kuch laanaa hai?

I'm going to the school, do you need anything?

✅ मैं बस थोड़ी देर दोस्त के यहां जा रहा हूँ।

Main bas thodi der dost ke yahaan jaa rahaa hoon.

I'm just going to my friend's place for a little while.

BONUS NOTE FOR LINGUISTIC CONTEXT :

In traditional Indian culture :

Grandparents are often co-residential (living in the same home).

Language is respectful, layered, and hierarchical.

- Use of "Aap", not "Tum."
- Children often speak formally, using honorifics like ji, e.g., Dadi ji, Aapne khana khaya?
- Storytelling and oral wisdom are frequent: "Jab main tumhari umar ka tha…"
- Code-switching between regional languages and Hindi/Urdu is common.
- There's often a lot of proverbs, idioms, and cultural reference embedded in speech
  (e.g., "boond boond se sagar bharta hai").

In Indian-American / diaspora families:

- Grandparents may be distant (video calls, short visits).
- Children may not be fluent in Hindi or regional languages, leading to:
- English mixed with Hindi, e.g., "Dadi, did you eat?" or "Aapko rice chahiye?"
- Sometimes "Tum" instead of "Aap" is used by mistake—not from disrespect but lack of cultural-linguistic context.
- Grandparent-grandchild relationships may rely more on ritual language (greetings, blessings) than deep daily conversation.

BUILD YOUR BILINGUAL LIBRARY WITH THESE BOOKS

A heartwarming story of set in an Indian wedding where a girl sees the beauty of our two worlds and the power of bilinguaism, beyond the accents and hesitation.

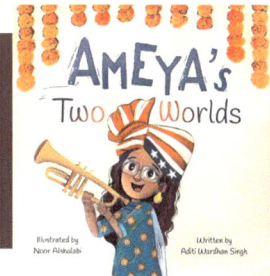

A great companion for this book is the alphabet book that helps kids understand the use and pronunciations of the Hindi alphabet using daily conversational sentences.

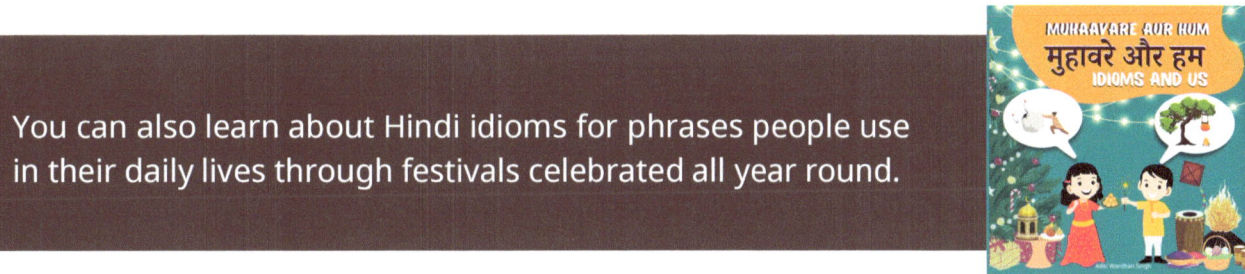

You can also learn about Hindi idioms for phrases people use in their daily lives through festivals celebrated all year round.

Bilingual Hindi English books that showcase the diversity and meaning behind these beautiful books.

About the Creator & Coach:

Aditi Wardhan Singh is a prolific writing coach, editor and multi-award-winning, bestselling author of fourteen inclusive books. Her experiences as a third culture child of Indian heritage raised in Kuwait, and challenges as a multicultural parent fuel her passion for diversifying dialogue around cultural awareness, identity and belonging. Her time spent volunteering as Hindi teacher and conducting cultural workshops at schools, shape her unique insight into the needs of the third culture child. She is also the founder and chief editor of the online and in print platform - **RaisingWorldChildren.com.**

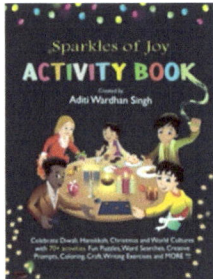

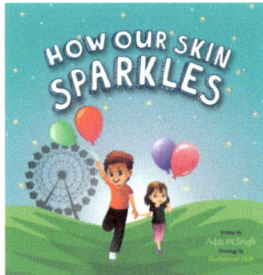

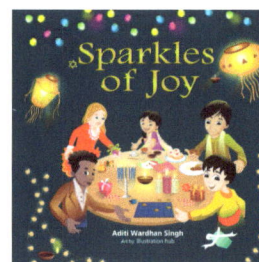

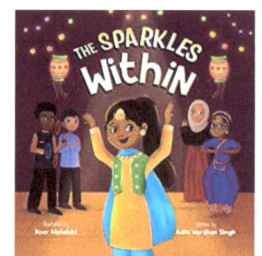

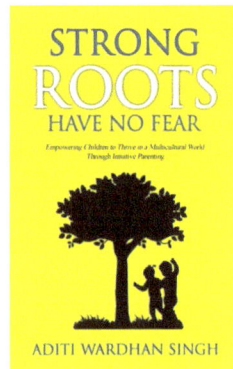

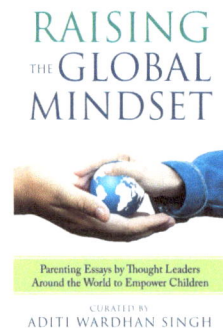

Book bundles include activity sheets & video read alouds

Thank you for taking a moment to review the book on Amazon or GoodReads.

Build confidence in self and belonging within...

www.ingramcontent.com/pod-product-compliance
Lightning Source LLC
LaVergne TN
LVHW072058070426
835508LV00002B/159